Color the Alphabet

Beautiful 17th Century Alphabet
Coloring Book for Adult Relaxation

By
I ♥ Coloring Books

Introduction

This alphabet is a stunning series of prints titled *Libellus Novus Elementorum Latinorum* designed by Polish goldsmith Jan Christian Bierpfaff and engraved by fellow-countryman Jeremias Falck between 1645 and 1650 and found in the **Rijksmuseum in Amsterdam.**

Use these beautiful letters to color and relax after a hard day's work, then you can frame your beautiful pieces and use them as monograms for your home or even as a gift.

You'll see two versions of the letter "A" but since the alphabet is old Dutch the letters "J" and "U" were never created.

I hope you enjoy these wonderfully detailed letters and take the opportunity to relax and create something beautiful.

I ♥ Coloring Books!

Color Test Page

Color Test Page

J. C. B. in: J. F. Sculp:

J.C.B. in: J.F. Sculp

J.C.B. in   J.F. Sculp:

J.C.B in: J.F. Sculp

J.C.B. in:

J.F. sculp:

J.C.Bir. in: J.F. Sculp:

J.C.B. in.   J.F. Sculp

J. C. B. in: J. F. Sculp:

J.C.B. in:

J.F. sculp:

J. C. B. in: J. F. Sculp:

J.C.B. in.   J.F. Sculp.

J. C. B. in: J. F. Sculp:

J.C.B. in: J.F. sculp:

Conclusion

I hope you've enjoyed *Color the Alphabet*, and if you did, I'd appreciate it if you would leave a review wherever you bought it – this really helps indie authors and artists like me.

Color me impressed!

I ♥ Coloring Books

www.ingramcontent.com/pod-product-compliance
Lightning Source LLC
Chambersburg PA
CBHW081115280526
45787CB00007B/2835